THE
GHOSTLY TALES
OF
ALBUQUERQUE

Published by Arcadia Children's Books
A Division of Arcadia Publishing
Charleston, SC
www.arcadiapublishing.com

Spooky America is a trademark of Arcadia Publishing, Inc.

First published 2021

Manufactured in the United States

ISBN: 978-1-4671-9839-4

Library of Congress Control Number: 2021938355

Notice: The information in this book is true and complete to the best of our knowledge. It is offered without guarantee on the part of the author or Arcadia Publishing. The author and Arcadia Publishing disclaim all liability in connection with the use of this book.

All images used courtesy of Shutterstock.com.

THE
GHOSTLY TALES
OF
ALBUQUERQUE

JESSA DEAN

Adapted from *Ghosts of Old Town Albuquerque* by Cody Polston

arcadia®
CHILDREN'S BOOKS

COLORADO

NEW MEXICO

ARIZONA

TEXAS

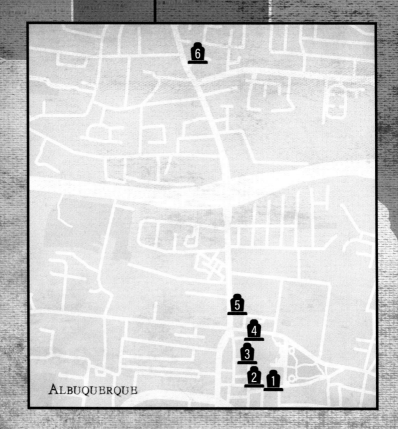

ALBUQUERQUE

TABLE OF CONTENTS & MAP KEY

Albuquerque, New Mexico

Introduction

Hungry for ghosts?

If you're reading this, ghosts are your thing. You may have watched all the ghost-hunting shows. You may have even read all the books about ghosts. But are you hungry for ghosts? I mean, *really* hungry? Because Albuquerque is ready to serve them up to you, and appropriately enough, restaurants are the best places to find them.

When you think of Albuquerque, you might picture the Old West, with cowboys striding down dusty roads in boots and spurs, gun at the ready for a shootout with an outlaw. The real Albuquerque isn't as dramatic as that, even if some areas looks like they could be part of a film set.

Even though it's busy with tourists, the Old Town area of Albuquerque seems pretty peaceful from the outside. Early settlers in the area erected adobe buildings that mimicked the

shape of the southwestern desert landscape, and those buildings still line the streets. Their long front porches offer rest and shade in the blistering heat. Many have been converted into museums and hotels, ready for tourists to explore. But there are also those like you who come to Albuquerque for the ghosts. Because when the sun goes down and the moon comes up, Albuquerque can be anything but peaceful when it comes to the paranormal.

The Spanish founded Albuquerque as a colony in 1706. Native Americans lived there long before that, and Mexican influence is just

as strong. The result is a mashup of cultures that gives the town a rich history. But like many old towns, Albuquerque has secrets buried under the surface. The thick adobe walls meant to keep enemies out kept a lot of spirits *inside* the old buildings. That makes it the perfect place for ghost hunters to spend time.

Everything in Old Town Albuquerque was once something else, and some of the former inhabitants aren't happy with the current uses of the places they once lived. But don't be too worried. Even the grumpy ghosts aren't vengeful as long as you respect them. Besides, you're just as likely to encounter a helpful ghost as one set on scaring you.

Trying to find a restaurant in Albuquerque that *doesn't* have ghosts is fairly difficult. Spirits seem to congregate at places where people like to gather and have fun. Some even try to participate.

So read on to find out just what to look out for in Albuquerque to make sure you have a spooky good time. After making your way through these pages, I'd be surprised if you didn't come back with a ghost story or two of your own to tell.

Ghosts on the Menu

La Placita Restaurant is just as notable for its history as for its food. The building formerly known as the Ambrosio Armijo House or Casa de Armijo was constructed between 1880 and 1882 and takes up a whole city block. It's known as one of the most haunted places in town. Rumor has it that at least four different ghosts haunt the Casa de Armijo. But there might be some confusion about where those ghosts actually reside. La Placita Restaurant was once known as La Hacienda. But for years, a restaurant named La Hacienda sat right next door to La Placita. So which restaurant do the ghostly tales actually belong to? Read on and decide for yourself!

Like many buildings in Old Town Albuquerque, Casa de Armijo was originally designed in the classic placita ("little plaza") style—the thick exterior walls made of adobe surrounded a small residential structure with a passageway and courtyard in the center. This unique structure made the residences more like fortresses, but the courtyard ensured those living there had beautiful surroundings. Many placitas had fountains and gardens in the courtyards. Some of the rooms were historically open-roof to let light and air in, so now one of the dining areas even has a huge cottonwood tree standing right in the middle of the room!

Unlike other buildings in Albuquerque, though, Casa de Armijo has an odd secret. The original owner, Ambrosio Armijo, added a second story to the traditional placita design. But it isn't usable. Ambrosio built it solely to please his daughter Teresa. Now it's the focus of much of the paranormal activity in the restaurant.

The story goes that Teresa's wedding dress had a long train of fabric trailing behind it. She wanted to show it off to her wedding guests. So her father ordered a beautiful walnut wood staircase from Spain just so Teresa could make a grand entrance in the courtyard before walking across the plaza to the church where she was married. There was no other real purpose to the second story of the house than to serve as a place for Teresa to begin her dramatic descent down the stairs on her wedding day.

Many believe Teresa is one of the ghosts who haunts the building because she's often found in the main hallway next to these antique stairs created specifically for her. But the ghost might not actually be Teresa. She could also be Teresa's sister Victoriana, who died (most likely during childbirth) at age 18, not long after she was married. Whichever sister haunts the building, she's never been seen alone. You'll only catch her with La Placita's youngest ghost by her side.

That ghost—known as Elizabeth—was only a little girl when she died sometime in the late 1800s, likely from tuberculosis, an infection that gets into the lungs and breaks down the body. She is believed to have been a servant girl. She appears wearing a formal white dress, her long black hair flowing. The beautiful dress has patterns of beadwork on the neck and shoulders, leading some to believe it was a first communion dress. For a long time, exact details of the dress were kept secret by ghost hunters. They would know someone had really seen Elizabeth if they could accurately describe the dress. Those familiar with the Pueblo Indians of the Albuquerque area are likely to recognize the patterns on Elizabeth's dress. The beadwork forms two large sun wheels on the shoulders and smaller ones on the hem and neckline. This is a traditional local motif.

In every way except the dress, Elizabeth looks just as real as you or me. She's not translucent the way you'd think a ghost would be. She doesn't glow or float or anything that would make you think "ghost." She appears as solid as one of us, tricking many people until she vanishes in an instant or runs through a wall.

Not everyone gets to see Elizabeth, though. She mostly appears only to kids and the elderly. You might spot her running around the restaurant or sitting in one of the dining rooms. But the best chance to meet her is in the women's bathroom since it used to be part of her bedroom. Even if you don't see her physical form standing there, keep a lookout. You might see her reflection behind you in the mirror while you wash your hands before dinner.

One story goes that during a wedding reception, two women saw Elizabeth sitting by herself in the corner and thought her parents had left her behind. When they went over to check on her, Elizabeth jumped up and ran down the hallway toward the restrooms. The women couldn't find her anywhere and worried she'd gotten lost. They scoured the restaurant looking for her and asked other guests and staff, but no one had seen a little girl. Eventually, they notified the restaurant manager. When the women described the girl, he said, "Don't worry. That's just one of our resident ghosts."

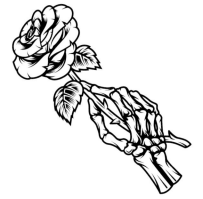

Elizabeth has been known to pull some pranks, such as tugging on the long skirts worn by waitresses and customers. But she's also learned some pretty scary tricks during her time as a ghost. She will often appear when someone is talking about her, especially if one of the people doesn't believe in ghosts. In theory, it sounds like daring her to show up would be a good way to see her. But I don't recommend it. One tour group got a demonstration from Elizabeth that can only be described as the stuff of nightmares.

If you've ever been on a ghost tour, you know that everyone is just waiting for something to happen. If you haven't, imagine you're standing in front of a restaurant that's supposed to be haunted. *Really* haunted. Nothing's happening, and you've been there awhile. Your feet hurt from all the walking on old streets. You're hungry and cranky and tired of hearing about ghosts without seeing any evidence. Then one shows up.

Someone points. Someone else screams. You look over and see a figure climbing the glass of one of the windows. Her limbs move like a spider's. Her white pajamas glow in the moonlight. Then she turns toward your group, and her face is hideous and distorted. Like something out of the pages of a horror comic.

What would you do? Would you freeze or run away in fear? Or would you enjoy the show?

One group had this exact experience and scattered across the plaza as soon as they saw Elizabeth. After they calmed down, several went back to their cars to leave. They had to walk past the window she had climbed. Their hearts beat faster as they walked past, but Elizabeth was long gone. Instead, a woman stood watching them through the dark window, even though the restaurant had closed long before.

It wasn't the only time Elizabeth climbed up the window. In 2004, eight people on a ghost tour got more than they bargained for when she appeared. She jumped up onto the window and climbed up to the roof. Once again, she appeared with her face distorted, looking like a demon of some kind. Most of the tourists ran in fear, but two stayed behind, excited to see an actual ghost. They refused to leave the area for hours, hoping to catch another glimpse. But Elizabeth was done for the night. She'd made her point.

Elizabeth is not the only ghost at La Placita who wants to put on a show. A spirit known to locals as George has become very good at mimicking voices. He loves to call out the restaurant staff by name. When they hear their names, they turn in the direction of the voice. No one is there. George once imitated one manager's voice so well, that the wait staff scrambled trying to carry out his orders. Later they found out he'd never given them! George especially likes to do his little tricks at shift changes to cause as much confusion as possible. If you visit La Placita, maybe you'll find him standing in the corner laughing at all the chaos. You can't really blame him, though. What else is a ghost going to do with its time?

Security guards patrol the streets Old Town Albuquerque at night, so they often spot ghosts at La Placita through the big front window. Standing on the street in the plaza outside the restaurant, the view goes straight through the window into the main hallway with Teresa's staircase at its center. One night after the restaurant had closed, a guard's headlights shone through the window, lighting up the hallway. He saw something odd, so he pulled over to investigate. But he couldn't see inside very well. The next day, he asked the manager if he'd rented out space in the building. He described what he saw: a woman holding a baby. She had looked directly at him and then moved out of sight. When he'd peered in through the windows, he couldn't find her. He assumed she belonged there since she hadn't set off the restaurant's alarm. The manager asked what she'd looked like, and the security guard pointed to a woman in one of the murals painted on the wall. You see, before most of it became a restaurant in the 1930s, the placita was made up of apartments and artist studios, including a well-known mural artist who painted realistic scenes from New Mexico. Whoever the woman in the mural was, she definitely wasn't standing in the restaurant that night.

In addition to the usual sightings of the resident ghosts, tourists and locals get to experience other strange, unexplained things at La Placita. While guiding a ghost tour outside one night, one man had his back to the restaurant's big front window. It was close to midnight. He began to tell some of the spooky stories you've just read. Suddenly, several people in his group screamed. He spun around and saw a large cloud of smoke moving away from the window near the staircase. The long-closed restaurant was dark. Those who saw what happened described our ghostly

friend Elizabeth in detail. So what *did* happen between the time they saw Elizabeth and the tour guide turned around?

Elizabeth had been sitting in a chair at the end of the hallway, and because she appeared solid, the tour group members assumed she was the child of an employee. They ignored her until she got up and walked toward the window. Once she stood exactly in front of the window, the thick cloud of smoke surrounded her and then seemed to swallow her whole! Can you imagine watching something like that happen? One minute, a little girl stands in front of the

window, and then she just dissolves into mist! It would be enough to keep you from sleeping for weeks!

Some paranormal investigators have tried to debunk the ghost tales of La Placita by explaining them as tricks of the light. They say headlights hitting the big front window refract through the warped glass and create a pattern that looks like the outline of a girl. It's true that over time, chemical cleaners used on window surfaces do degrade and stain the glass. So it's possible that headlights could create a strange trick of the light that looks like the outline of a person. But that explanation doesn't quite fit.

In 2005, a tour employee tried to pull a prank. To scare the tourists, he was going to station himself inside the restaurant in front of the window. He planned to hit the glass at the exact moment the guide told one of the ghost stories. But he hit too hard and broke the window. The glass had to be replaced with flat, modern glass without any warps. Now skeptics can't use the headlight explanation anymore. But that's not the only reason attempts to debunk the hauntings don't fly. The headlight explanation doesn't work for a number of other experiences people have had inside the restaurant through the years. Paranormal investigators have documented supernatural activity at Casa de Armijo using more than just eyewitness testimony.

One such study by investigators tested fourteen locations in the Southwest that were rumored to be haunted. Their theory was that introducing positive ions into the air could potentially result in conditions that would make it more likely for paranormal activity to occur. You see, paranormal investigators have found that ghosts appear more often when the air is charged with energy. There are negative and positive ions in all of the air you breathe, but there are more in outdoor locations than indoor spots. Locations near water have an even greater concentration, since wind and water movement create friction, stirring up the ions in the air.

To study this theory, investigators placed several machines known as a positive ion generators in the fourteen spots, including La Placita. These high-powered generators forced positive ions into the air to produce the exact conditions they believed would attract spirits. It worked, in theory. Only two locations out of the fourteen showed activity. La Placita was one.

They placed infrared cameras throughout the area around Teresa's staircase, which is where many of ghost sightings take place. Infrared cameras show ghosts better than regular cameras, since they capture temperatures. Humans are warm. Ghosts aren't.

While they watched, bright flashes of light appeared out of nowhere. The lights moved around the staircase and then disappeared. The investigators determined that the source of light was at the top of the staircase, but they couldn't figure what caused it. But they got what they wanted: lots of evidence of increased paranormal activity after the ion generators were used.

These same investigators also used special equipment to obtain two recordings of electronic voice phenomena or EVP. Ghost hunters use EVP to capture frequencies our ears can't hear, and they often report recording voices that could only be from spirits.

The theory is that since spirits can't speak, they manipulate sound to mimic the human voice. That's why the content can be scrambled or incomplete.

In the recordings taken at Casa de Armijo, investigators heard the names Victoria and Elizabeth underneath all the background noise in a scratchy, unidentifiable voice. They weren't surprised about either name. Years before, a psychic had predicted that Victoriana, Ambrosio's other daughter, was one of the ghosts haunting La Placita.

Investigators concluded that the hallway really is the ghost "hotspot" of the restaurant, as many employees and witnesses have claimed. It makes sense. While resident ghost George seems to drift around the restaurant, the other spirits mostly appear in that area. That makes it a sure place to encounter a ghost when you visit. You might want to have your camera ready to capture one of the ghosts on film. Hopefully Elizabeth won't put on her demon face and instead let you chase her around the dining room!

A Mansion of the Unexplained

Remember that La Placita used to be called La Hacienda? And that there was *another* La Hacienda right next door, leaving people confused about which ghosts belong where? Well, that neighboring property has plenty of its own stories. You won't find it under the name La Hacienda anymore, though. After many years, its name was recently changed to Hacienda del Rio Cantina. But the ghosts haven't changed, so it's the next stop on our journey through spooky Albuquerque. The restaurant occupies the former Blueher Mansion, built on the site of an ancient adobe building that once housed Army officers. Think one or two of them stuck around? Let's find out.

Additions and renovations to the building through the years seem to have disturbed some of its former occupants, making them more likely to pull pranks and make things difficult for the restaurant staff. Oddly enough, a lot of the ghostly activity here also centers around an old staircase. Both employees and customers have heard voices and laughter near the staircase, seemingly drifting down from the third floor. But the third floor has long been sealed off to the public by a gate built directly onto the stairs. No one should be able to enter who isn't authorized to be there.

One night, a manager and some customers stood at the foot of the stairs and heard activity above them. The manager assumed some customers had bypassed the gate to explore upstairs. He searched the entire third floor but found no one there. No one came down the stairs, either.

Ghostly noises don't just come from the third floor, though. One night after they closed the restaurant, a manager and employee were hanging out in the break room on the third floor before heading home. They heard something that sounded like muffled conversations and a gentle piano tune coming from the stairwell. Knowing they were the only two people in the restaurant (the only two *alive*, anyway), they slowly descended the stairs. When they reached the first floor, they found it completely dark and empty. Our brave employees shrugged it off and went back upstairs. But as soon as they got to the third floor, the noise started up again. This time they ran downstairs, as fast as they could, only to find nothing. It didn't take them long to leave after that!

Phantom music is pretty common at the restaurant. But the resident ghosts have other favorite pranks that both scare and delight employees and customers. They turn things upside down, open doors, and toss dishes around. Employees hear footsteps behind them and someone calling their names when no one is around. One spirit even likes to run straight at the waitstaff with hard, heavy steps, hoping to scare them. A waitress who previously didn't believe in ghosts now does and calls "her" ghost Jose. She always says goodnight to him when she shuts down the restaurant, just in case.

Several employees and customers have even seen ghosts in the restaurant. One is an unidentified woman who seems harmless enough and doesn't bother people. Another is a little boy who likes to join customers in the dining room. One evening, the restaurant was empty, and a couple came in for dinner. A waitress told them to sit wherever they liked. She noticed a little boy next to them, so she brought three glasses of water and three sets of silverware into the dining room. But when she approached the table, the boy wasn't there. She asked where he'd gone and got confused responses. They weren't sure whether the waitress was seeing things or whether the restaurant was haunted!

Records show that the restaurant has been haunted for a very long time. The oldest-known ghost story there comes from 1958, when a waitress named Frances shared her story in an interview for a government project. Each morning, she and the other waitresses would have coffee together before starting their shift. One day, she entered the restaurant around 6:00 a.m. and headed back to the coffee area to prepare the coffee. She didn't notice anything odd at first. Then she spotted a cup sitting on the table where the waitresses gathered each morning. It already had coffee in it.

Frances assumed the cup was left over from the night before and reached for it to dump it out. She touched her finger to the coffee, and it was hot. The cup, however, was cold. She left it there and ran to get the cook to show him. But when they got back to the table, the cup had vanished. The cook hadn't brought coffee, and the machine clearly hadn't made any. So who was drinking that cup of coffee that morning?

It seems Frances's ghost left a mess for her to clean up, but do you think maybe her ghost just wanted to join in on the coffee and gossip with the other waitresses? How would you feel about having a ghostly companion as a coworker? I doubt it would scare a brave ghost hunter like you. And hey, maybe the ghost might even help you clean up like one did at this very haunted place!

In 1960, a carpenter worked on the third floor, chiseling old paint off of the window frames. Each time he'd set his tools down and look away, he'd turn back to find the tools had been hung up on the wall, a few feet away. He smelled perfume each time it happened, so eventually, he just followed his nose to find the tools.

Current employees aren't surprised by these stories. They all agree that there's always

a ghostly presence at this restaurant. Most believe at least two or three spirits haunt the place. One appears to be the ghost of a Spanish soldier who lived and died there. He keeps to himself, watching over everything calmly and never getting angry or rude.

Employees have also seen a girl near the second-floor storage room. There's even a ghost they call Mary, who has appeared to many people who have worked at or visited the restaurant. Mary actually worked there herself around 1980, and her story is a sad one. She had been dating a local gangster. When she broke it off, he showed up at the restaurant's back door that night, demanding to see her. He pounded on the door and became violent. The kitchen staff called the police and sent someone to the gift shop to warn Mary. But before they could warn her, she clocked out for the end of her shift and went outside. Her boyfriend spotted her and pulled out a pistol. He shot Mary twice before shooting himself. Both died together by the old tree behind the restaurant.

It's no surprise that Mary still hangs around after such an awful death. Many customers spot her in the restaurant, still cleaning and serving drinks like she did while she was alive. She often moves drinks out of the way to wipe down tables. You can see the liquid from her dishrag on the surface of the table. Despite Mary's tragic end, she's still trying to be helpful.

Several spirits come from the time when the property was known as Blueher Mansion. One of the former inhabitants stuck around long after her home became a restaurant. Sophie Blueher likes to drift through walls wearing her old-fashioned dress. Guests have said she brings a peaceful, calming energy when she passes by, but they also can feel some sadness in her. An elderly man in old-fashioned clothes also shows up sometimes at the top

of the antique staircase. Maybe he's also one of the Blueher family, although no one can confirm that.

Other ghosts may not appear in physical form in the restaurant, but there's no mistaking their presence. The second floor seems to be a hotspot for these undead residents of this haunted spot. One waitress tells of investigating flickering lights on the second floor, only to find that her reflection in a mirror had morphed into that of an old woman. Others have reported children crying and footsteps and furniture scraping across the floor.

One thing is for sure about this haunted restaurant: when you visit, chances are good you'll have an experience you just can't explain. Whether it's having your water glass refilled by a ghost or hearing the phantom piano play, keep an eye and ear out. Your story might be the next one told through the years.

The Temperamental Ghost

Another Albuquerque restaurant with more than its share of permanent ghosts is the Church Street Cafe, also known as Casa de Ruiz. It was supposedly built just after the city was founded in 1706, so the hacienda has seen a little bit of everything both inside and outside its walls. The U-shaped residence was built from *terrones*, a type of adobe brick made from river bottom dirt, more than two feet thick in places! Back when it was built, it stood on a marshy swamp flooded with waters from the nearby Rio Grande River.

Even though it's called Casa de Ruiz, there's strangely no record of the Ruiz family living here until 130 years after the hacienda was built. Rufina, the last member of the Ruiz family, died in 1991 at the age of 91. It's said that strong Mexican families don't let what belongs to them go easily. Since generations of the family lived in the dwelling, it wouldn't be surprising to find a few who weren't quite ready to say goodbye to Casa Ruiz's walls.

It's believed that a previous resident, Sarah Ruiz, haunts the hacienda, even now. She was a very unique woman during the lifetime, serving as a *curandera,* or healer, in the community. She would have used medicinal herbs, mysticism, and energy work to heal—things that weren't very common in the 1900s. Some outsiders might have even labeled her as a witch, even though she followed traditional practices.

The current owner of the building, Marie Coleman, met Sarah not long after she purchased the residence. Marie had workers making repairs to the damaged building. One day, as she entered the building with a contractor, a distinctive, loud, female voice shouted from behind her. The voice insisted the contractor leave. Marie felt the air grow thicker with anger as she and the contractor moved through the building. Once she rushed him out the door, the air returned to peaceful calm. Several years later, Marie learned that the contractor was related to someone Sarah Ruiz disliked intensely.

Marie instead brought in a friend of hers to finish the job, but that didn't go smoothly either. After a couple hours of work, her friend came to her frustrated and demanded that Marie do something about "that woman." Sarah had been kicking the buckets of stucco around so that the workers were unable to do any repairs on the building. Marie was stunned. She hadn't told anyone about the demanding ghost, and now another contractor had reported a similar experience. Marie walked to the construction area and simply asked Sarah to let the men work so they could fix up her home. After that, the work continued peacefully. It seems Sarah just wanted to protect what had been hers.

Since then, the two women have formed a good relationship. Marie greets Sarah every time she enters the restaurant in the morning and says goodbye at night. If Marie forgets to say goodnight to Sarah, the lights will turn on and off until Marie comes back inside. When

Sarah wants her attention during the day, she throws pebbles at Marie. These aren't just any pebbles. They don't come from the area and are kept in a glass jar underneath the cash register. That way, everyone knows it's really Sarah causing a fuss.

Before you think this is all in Marie's head, many people in the restaurant have seen Sarah's behavior for themselves, and some have even seen Sarah! One of the waiters describes her as an older woman in a long, black dress with jet-black hair pulled into a bun. She's often spotted doing household chores such as sweeping or dusting, still taking care of Casa de Ruiz. And as you've already seen, she's very particular about her home.

On one Sunday afternoon, a Spanish guitar player performed at the restaurant. In front of a full audience, a coffee cup levitated off of a table during one of his songs. It slammed into a wall, crashing to the floor in little pieces. To this day, the guitar player won't play that particular song, no matter how much you ask him. Sarah must *really* have hated that tune!

But that wasn't the guitar player's only experience with Sarah. A few years later, he relayed some of the stories to his girlfriend. Not believing him, she decided to go check it out for herself. After the couple finished eating and prepared to leave, the restaurant went completely dark in an instant—not only the overhead lights, but also all electrical devices and lights in the merchandise cases. The second the girlfriend walked out the door, the lights turned back on.

Sarah likes to play these kinds of jokes on those who don't believe in ghosts. Marie's skeptical brother visited once and left a believer. He'd come to help Marie when she opened the restaurant. The first night he closed up alone, he confirmed everything had been turned off and was ready to leave, but he couldn't find the keys. He was locked inside the restaurant. He looked all over the place, even getting down on his knees to search the bathroom floor. From that position, he heard a woman laughing. "Sarah, leave me alone," he called out. Then he stood up, and his keys jangled in his pocket. But he couldn't dismiss what had happened so easily. When he went to the front door, it was wide open. You can bet he's a believer now!

Lights and small objects aren't the only things Sarah enjoys messing with. One of her favorite things to do is move merchandise around in the restaurant. One display case contains figurines and pottery. During the

night, Sarah moves the items and places them in different positions. Due to the way the figurines are positioned, it seems that she's often recreating a scene of something that happened in her life. But it's not as funny as it sounds. Sometimes she moves them dangerously close to the edges of the shelves. Marie has tried reasoning with Sarah many times, but nothing has worked. Instead, Sarah has sometimes thrown figurines against the glass of the case so hard that Marie feared both would break. Eventually, Marie put larger pieces of pottery at the edges of the shelves to keep the other smaller objects from falling off. Sarah doesn't seem to have the ability to move those.

Sarah does love putting on a show for a bit of fun, but her temper flares when people talk about painful parts of her life. A TV ghost show was filming on the patio one day, and some paranormal investigators stopped by to see the action. The show had been reenacting a fight Sarah had with the man she loved. A fight that involved a knife. While the crew filmed, something happening inside the restaurant. The ghost hunters hurried to check it out.

Silverware covered the floor, and several customers were pressed against the wall. Witnesses said the silverware had flown off the tables as if someone had grabbed it and hurled it to the floor. Over a dozen people witnessed the shocking incident. According to Marie, Sarah especially hates people bringing up that fight, so the flying silverware was to make them change the subject.

While Sarah can be a handful at times, generally, she's a welcome presence. Marie has gotten used to her being there, and many come to Church Street specifically to hear stories of Sarah. This resident ghost stands ready to welcome you, fellow ghost hunter. But make sure not to bring any unbelievers around. Sarah might give them the scare of their lives!

Showdown at High Noon

The High Noon Restaurant is located partially inside one of the original structures of Old Town Albuquerque, built in 1785. This building has housed many enterprises through the years, including a gambling casino and a woodworking shop. At the turn of the nineteenth century, it was even home to nuns! Many people have passed through the building throughout the centuries, and some of them liked it so much, they decided to stay. One male and one female spirit are especially well-known to visitors and patrons of the restaurant. Let's get to know them.

The male ghost has been absent for long periods of the building's history. Some believe he was a trapper and that he keeps the schedule a trapper would kept have during the pioneer days of the town. A trapper would have been going off to track animals with companies who used the fur and meat. Sometimes his travels would take him far away for weeks at a time before he could come home. If he's walking in the footsteps of his life, it explains his long absences. But when the ghost decides to show back up again, there's no mistaking his presence. He rattles dishes and calls out the employees' names. He even flushes toilets randomly, and sometimes he pinches ladies in the restroom. Maybe someone should pinch him back and teach him a lesson!

Several psychics have visited the High Noon, and they declared that the ghost's name is Frank. It's believed he was robbed and murdered in the building. But don't be so quick to believe it. After the staff started referring to him as Frank, the ghost confronted a regular customer. He blocked the man's way and shouted, "My name is not Frank!" So maybe it's best not to call him that when you visit, unless you want an angry fur trapper after you!

The female ghost is more of a mystery. No one is sure who she is. After the restaurant is closed, employees often hear her talking in one of the main rooms. They speculate that she lived there when it was a home or worked there when it was a casino. One employee says she wears a formal dress. When she appeared one

Christmas Eve, she had on an old-fashioned dress that would have been worn by someone in mourning after a loved one died. Many people don't realize this woman is a ghost until they notice her clothing and how still she remains. She often just sits peacefully, as if waiting for someone or something.

Customers and employees have had encounters with the two ghosts on many occasions. They've been tapped on their shoulders with no one around. Some have been knocked down by a force as they exit a door, like they ran into someone, only to realize there's no one there. People often hear the phantom sound of a pair of boots with spurs walking across a wood floor in an older section of the restaurant. Once the ghostly boots reach the newer part of the restaurant, the sound stops, as if the ghostly shoes can't cross the line between the old and the new.

The resident ghosts at the High Noon have also shown themselves a few times. After all the customers had left one night, and the bartender was closing up, she spotted a tall figure in a robe or cloak. She assumed it was a customer who'd accidentally been locked inside. When she grabbed the keys to let him out, the entryway stood empty, and the door was still locked. No one could have exited without her noticing.

Staff say that same entryway is a good place to spot the male ghost because it's in the old part of the building. Late at night, many employees have felt someone watching them and noticed movement out of the corner of their eyes. They sense a man looking through the window at them. When they turn to look, the man vanishes. The bar is also a good area to catch a ghost. But hold onto your soda—drinks have been known to "jump" off the counter!

High Noon's ghosts really love to move things around in the restaurant, so it's best to keep an eye out in every room, just to be safe. One waitress had a scare one night after she had let everyone else go home. As she turned off the lights and restaurant equipment, she heard a strange noise behind her. Spinning around, she found all of the plates that had been lined up on the cook's preparation table had been moved. When she got closer for a look, the plates moved again, right before her eyes. She watched the table shake violently, causing the plates to jump and crash down to the floor. You can't really blame her for not wanting to close by herself anymore! Would you work alone if you'd seen that?

Another hot spot for paranormal activity at the High Noon is the fireplace area, so you'll definitely want to check it out if you visit. It sits between the newer and older parts of the building, and most of the unexplained occurrences have happened nearby. Sometimes you'll smell a strong odor of smoke even though there's no fire burning. You can imagine how stressful that can get for the restaurant's staff! In fact, phantom smoke smells are so frequent that they try to determine the cause of the smell before they call the fire department. One Christmas Eve, the smoke even smelled like piñon, a type of pine tree in the area that's often used to make a fire smell especially wonderful. It was as if the dead were celebrating the holiday along with the living.

The ghosts don't limit themselves to the inside of the restaurant, though. Even the parking lot of the High Noon is haunted! Many have spotted a ghostly nun in her official black and white habit wandering the parking area. She seems to be looking for something. When approached, she vanishes into thin air.

Whether you hang out in the dining room or the parking lot, you're likely to have an experience you can't explain at the High Noon.

Just be careful. The last thing you want is to make a ghost mad. It might turn into a standoff like in an old western movie!

Strange Dining Companions

For years, one of the most popular romantic restaurants in Albuquerque also happened to be the most haunted. The Maria Teresa Restaurant operated in a beautiful building erected in 1783, formerly known as the Salvador Armijo House. The restaurant closed in 2004, and the Hotel Albuquerque purchased the building. The hotel recently turned it into a private event space called Casa Esencia after it sat empty for years. The new purpose doesn't change anything but the way it looks. The ghosts remain.

The centerpiece of the building is a long bar that was moved in 1970 to the former restaurant from Fort Sumner, about two-and-a-half hours away. What's so special about this bar? Well, have you ever heard of the famous outlaw Billy the Kid and his gang of robbers? They used to drink at that very bar in between gunfights and stealing cattle. They grabbed cold drinks and told stories, while laughing and daring anyone

to arrest them. Billy the Kid may have become famous, but the ghosts of the Salvador Armijo House are the ones we want to meet.

Whether it's the bar or the building itself, the restaurant attracts spirits. At least four distinct ghostly images have been spotted there. Both employees and customers report encounters, and weirdly, most of them didn't even know the place was haunted!

Typical for houses at the time, the hacienda that houses the restaurant was originally made up of twelve rooms, each opening onto a central patio or placita. The placita held stables for horses, a water well, and storage rooms. On the east, south, and north sides, covered passageways called *zaguanes* allowed covered wagons to enter the placita. It would basically be like having a driveway and garage in the middle of your house!

Residences like these were designed for defense. During colonial times, the Spanish built their homes like forts, allowing the occupants to gather in the center with everything they needed to be able to withstand attack. The walls were plastered with layers of mud, inside and out. In fact, the original walls of the Salvador Armijo House were almost three feet thick!

Years of changes in ownership to all or a portion of the house resulted in many renovations, but the house is still mostly intact. When the home was used as a restaurant, guests entered through the remains of the original placita. Each of the original twelve rooms was named after the families who once lived there. Some of the family members still do.

The Armijo Room is a popular spot for ghosts to appear, so it's the first stop in our investigation. Waiters working in the old restaurant found that when they arrived at a table to take an order, a woman in a white beaded dress had beaten them to it. Only problem? The female staff didn't wear white; they wore maroon dresses. Customers

described the woman as Latina and around fifty years old. She had dark hair with grey streaks in it, pulled up in a bun. Many believe her to be Maria de las Nieves Sarracineo.

She was the second wife of Salvador Armijo, the man who built the hacienda. The couple became very wealthy, building a property empire in Albuquerque. But they had a very troubled marriage. The already difficult Maria became even colder and more ruthless as she grew older. It didn't help that financial difficulties began to eat away at their empire, and family fights over money resulted in lawsuits. By the time she died in 1898, her fortune was nearly gone, and her legacy was in ruins. So it's probably not surprising that she has unfinished business she wants to stick around for.

No one is sure why she spends so much time in that particular room, but during its restaurant days, she frequently tried to take dessert orders there. One Easter Sunday, a headwaiter named Daniel arrived at a table to find she'd done it again. Only this time, she'd actually been pushing a dessert cart, loaded with plates of sweet treats. Sounds helpful, until you find out that the restaurant didn't have a dessert cart!

Maria also likes to visit the room that was formerly referred to as the Wine Press. But she's usually spotted in or near the women's restrooms. You have to be quick to get a glimpse of her. She tends to move through quickly, followed by a cold burst of air. Usually, the only way to detect her presence is a chilling feeling of being watched.

If you get the opportunity to peek inside Casa Esencia looking for Maria, you might actually encounter another ghost. One of the rooms held an antique piano, and one of the resident spirits loved to play haunting tunes late at night. In fact, the first time it happened in 1987, the night manager was closing up and thought a burglar had snuck in! He quietly moved to lock the door, hoping to trap the person while he waited for police. The officers came in, weapons drawn and flashlights blazing, only to find no one there and nothing out of place. It's not clear if the antique piano

remains, but I bet the ghost finds a way to make his music regardless.

Our favorite former headwaiter, Daniel, encountered the invisible piano player late one night after everyone else had gone. He was doing paperwork in the lobby when he heard soft music. He checked each room, stumbling around in the dark to reach the light switch. The moment he entered the Armijo Room to turn on the lights, the music stopped. The room stood empty.

So far, you've met helpful and entertaining ghosts at Casa Esencia. But not all of the

resident ghosts like their home being used by others. When the building served as a restaurant, employees encountered frustrating situations in which their work was undone, sometimes in dangerous ways. Waitresses tell of placing silverware on all the tables after closing, only to come in later to find it had been moved. Often, the silverware had been dumped into a big pile on one of the tables. Harmless pranks, right? Sure. But one prank turned scary when a waitress entered the room with a full tray of water glasses to place on a table. The moment she crossed into the room, the glasses began to explode one by one. Shards of glass rained down onto the table, the customers, and their food. Luckily no one was seriously injured!

There's another ghost who specifically disliked the waitstaff so much that they referred to the ghost as the "waiter hater." The ghost's identity is unknown, but it had some connection to a portrait that hung in the Armijo Room during the restaurant days. The portrait is of an Armijo family member with unusual light eyes that seem to follow you as you move throughout the room. The ghost might be that of the person in the portrait or someone who cared about them. Either way, the waiter hater dislikes when people talk badly about the painting. It started with one waiter who disliked working in the Armijo Room both because of the portrait and the room's energy. When forced to work in the room, he would make rude comments and jokes about the portrait.

Soon, other staff noticed a pattern. Anytime the waiter said something nasty about the portrait, something bad happened to him. He'd been a great employee when he started, with a solid history of work at other restaurants. But he became clumsy, making mistakes such as dropping trays of food and knocking over glasses when the room was full of diners. You can probably guess where this happened. That's right, exactly in front of the portrait. Tensions finally came to a breaking point one night when an unseen hand shoved him to the ground as he passed by the portrait. You won't be surprised to hear that he quit his job right after that!

Many employees encountered our next ghost, but you have to search him out if you want to meet him. He sits in the Chacon Room, which had a large mirror on the west wall. The man wears a dark suit with a white collared shirt and has a full head of dark gray hair. He keeps his arms at his side and merely sits, as if waiting for someone. He's clearly visible, solid as can be, but only if you look in the mirror on the wall. The spot he occupies in the room appears vacant otherwise.

Another antique mirror inside was well-known in Albuquerque for being haunted. It hung in a small dining room called the Zamora Room. One day, a waitress took the order of a table of six directly under the mirror. She walked away to give the order to the kitchen. One of the guests rushed up to her. "How do you do that?" she asked and excitedly mentioned the restaurant's entertainment. The confused waitress followed her back into the dining room. Clearly visible in the mirror was a seventh person, sitting between two of the actual guests. The woman was in her thirties with long, black hair, a slim face, and hazel eyes. She wore a white dress with long sleeves and jewelry.

The diners assumed it was some special effect to entertain guests. Not wanting to alarm the guests, the waitress played along. Over the next hour, employees snuck into the room to get a peek at the ghostly visitor without alerting the guests that anything was wrong. They'd fill water glasses or clean a table, all to catch a glimpse. As the dinner progressed, the ghost seemed to participate in the fun. She moved her arms and hands regularly and took an interest in each plate of food. The staff got the impression she was concerned that customers feel taken care of and have a nice time. But once the waitress came in to offer dessert, the ghost completed her task. The diners noticed the woman slowly disappearing in the mirror.

A different lady made her presence known in the Sarachino Room, a cozy dining room next to the Armijo Room. She is a middle-aged Latina woman with light-colored eyes and dark hair wearing a beautiful red dress. This lady in red leaves behind the scent of flowery perfume as she passes. Some have heard her ask for help only to find no one there. Others have seen her in the doorway. She enters, stares at the people who notice her, and then vanishes. Maybe she's looking for the man in the dark suit, but she has only ever been spotted in the Sarachino Room and the Wine Press room.

Why do you think so many ghosts haunt this particular building? After all, many buildings in Albuquerque are older, and I haven't told you about any murders or battles fought there. We can guess that maybe the former inhabitants just really liked living there! Or maybe something more sinister is at work. When ghosts are involved, it's just as likely to be one as the other, and Casa Esencia is no exception.

In 1993, water pipes under the floor of the bar had to be replaced, and while digging, workers made a gruesome discovery. A stack of bones (from both humans and horses) lay deep under the building. They appeared to have been there for many years. Could they belong to some of the former inhabitants of the Salvador Armijo House? Is that the reason the ghosts stuck around? Maybe not, since the resident ghosts haven't exactly left since the bones were dug up.

And what about Billy the Kid? Has he ever shown up at the bar brought over from Fort Sumpter? Maybe. In October 2000, a diner at a table in the bar saw a man dressed in

western wear standing in the doorway of the bar. His wife couldn't see the cowboy, but the man swears he was there. A couple years later, another guest seated at the same table saw the cowboy, again standing in the doorway. Neither one of them knew the restaurant was haunted. So maybe Billy did tag along with the bar he loved to hang out at. With his outlaw days behind him, he might be happy now to let the other ghosts of the hacienda get all the attention.

Ghost History Lessons

No one's sure when the building known as Las Mañanitas was erected, but legend says that some sections are at least three hundred years old. Because there have been so many additions and changes over the years, the building resembles a patchwork quilt, pieced together by many hands. You can tell which parts were added at different times and by which owners. It's been closed for several years. Meanwhile, the ghosts wait inside for someone to reopen it, and you know they will.

It was once a stagecoach stop on the El Camino Real road that ran through the valley to Santa Fe, New Mexico. Drivers would rest themselves and their horses before continuing on their journey. Later it served as a pool hall and bar. It even became a farm and blacksmith shop at one point. Recent owners have found pieces of iron from that time period on the property.

Most recently, beginning in 1985, Las Mañanitas has been home to a couple of restaurants. When a couple named Paul and Linda bought the place, they learned it was haunted. Since then, the ghosts have appeared to them many times. But the ghosts there are inconsistent. Some months there will be no paranormal activity at all—then something will set off the ghosts for several days in a row.

A previous owner of the building had the worst of it. She believed that evil spirits haunted her. Plates would fly at her out of the oven. As soon as she walked through a door, it would slam behind her. This stressed her out so much that she removed all doors within the building. Determined to get rid of these evil spirits, she even got help from members of a local church to perform an exorcism! During an exorcism, a Catholic priest performs a ceremony designed to drive demons out of a living human. I'm not sure if it ever works with banishing undead things. It certainly didn't stop the ghosts at Las Mañanitas!

But some of the ghosts can be bribed to be on good behavior. When Paul and Linda took over, staff of the restaurant that previously operated there told them to leave toys out. A ghost boy and girl can often be seen playing on the patio. You can also sometimes hear them playing in the house. As long as they have toys, they don't bother anyone. So Linda hid toys for them in different areas, out of view of the customers. Bizarrely, when she looked for the toys later, they were always broken. Paul and Linda's cat often appeared to be playing chase with the kids in the hallways, so at least someone enjoyed their presence!

Other ghosts in the building like to get people's attention. Paul and Linda have seen the metal chandelier in the dining room swing back and forth so forcefully, they worried it would rip out of the ceiling! You can't even say the wind or air conditioning were to blame. Everything had been turned off, and there wasn't even a light breeze that night.

Diners in the same room often saw things fly in and out of the fireplace. Described as a cloud or a ball of smoke, it would shoot out of the fireplace into the center of the room before disappearing. Lights in the dining room also go on and off without warning, especially at night. What's weirder,

though, is that the lights have a dial switch. Paul will turn it to the off position and later come back to find the lights on even though the dial hasn't moved.

You may have heard that cold spots indicate ghosts, and we talked earlier about how they don't generate heat. Las Mañanitas has a lot of cold spots, which indicates the supernatural activity is especially high. Many employees have experienced this over the years. Even though the temperature inside the building gets very hot due to Albuquerque's climate, the cold spots remain.

In the room Paul and Linda used for an office, they often heard what sounded like the squeaking of a rocking chair, even though nothing like that was in the room. When a psychic visited the restaurant once, she asked to look around. She went into the office. Without knowing about the couple's experiences, the psychic described it as a sewing room with a rocking chair.

The same psychic told Paul and Linda that a man had been hanged in one of the older rooms at the back of the building. The owners had never heard of a murder or death of any kind in the building, but it would possibly explain at least one of the restaurant's more helpful permanent guests.

Paul recalls one day when he and an employee cooked for a huge crowd at lunchtime. A waitress complained they'd run out of clean coffee cups, but no one had time to wash them. Shortly after, Paul heard the dishwasher running and dishes rattling in the sink. He assumed Linda had gone to the back to do the work, even though she was supposed to be out front helping customers. But then she walked into the kitchen from the dining room. So who was washing dishes? Both Linda and the other employee heard the noises in the dishwasher area, too. When they checked, no one was there. However, they did find that all the coffee cups had been washed and placed on the drying rack for them.

The restaurant wasn't advertised as haunted, but that didn't stop guests from figuring it out on their own. Out of the blue, customers would ask staff about ghosts. They described feeling some kind of presence and just "knowing" that the restaurant was haunted. In fact, one man felt so uncomfortable that he went out to his car to wait for his wife to finish her dinner because he couldn't bear to be inside anymore!

So what do we know about the ghosts of Las Mañanitas? Not a whole lot. A photographer did capture a portrait of one, though. In one of the photos she took around the property, you can see a grandmother and her cat faintly in the background. However, every time the photographer has returned to try to duplicate the moment, her photos all turn out black.

Paul and Linda believe there are only two main ghosts who haunt the building. The first they call Priscilla, and she leaves a strong impression. Not only can you feel her presence in the room, but the distinct smell of her perfume drifts throughout the restaurant. It's so strong, customers have even complained about it! Priscilla has appeared several times,

but she vanishes quickly after being spotted. A mariachi (a musician who plays traditional Mexican music) spotted her in a big white gown. A busboy once saw a blond-haired woman believed to be Priscilla entering the men's bathroom. He waited for her to exit and then knocked on the door. After no answer, he tried the doorknob, but it was locked. Eventually, he knocked again with no answer. This time when he tried the door, it was unlocked, but no one was in the room.

The second ghost is the complete opposite of the first. Linda describes him as a young man who is very big—so big that you can't miss

him out of the corner of your eye. She often got him mixed up with one of the male employees and called out to him before realizing he wasn't really there. This ghost can get a little too friendly, though. Linda had to warn new female employees to not freak out if they felt a touch on their shoulder or hip and no one was around.

There may actually be a connection between these two ghosts that would make a lot of sense. A young niece of a regular customer reported communicating with a boy under the floor in the bathroom. She had never heard the stories of the young man walking around the restaurant. After many encounters with him, she finally learned his name: Joaquin. Joaquin happens to be the name of Priscilla's child. She died while giving birth to him on site. Many believe that the two of them wander Las Mañanitas trying to find each other, missing each other by just a little bit since neither knows what the other looks like. Maybe you can try to help them find each other if you get a chance to visit. It would be nice for them to be together after all this time. They might even be able to finally rest in peace.

So Many Ghosts, So Little Time

Our ghostly tour of Albuquerque has come to an end, but the fun doesn't need to stop here! The ghosts are just waiting for you to visit. Late at night, when the moon is high in the sky, take a walk around Old Town Albuquerque. Peek in the windows of the old buildings. Linger a while in the plaza and wait for something completely unexplained to happen. You never know what—or who—you might spot lurking around in the mist (or even climbing up the windows)!

Ask the restaurant employees to tell you tales of their spooky encounters. Take one of the many ghost tours. See what new stories you can find to add to what you've seen here, since we've barely scratched the surface of

spooky Albuquerque. You may even want to get out your ghost hunting equipment so you can track down spirits outside of Old Town. In a city this old, the supernatural lurks around every corner if you pay attention.

Chances are, if you seek out ghosts in Albuquerque, you'll find them. If they don't find you first.

Jessa Dean writes spooky stories for kids and has been a ghostwriter for multiple authors who unfortunately don't write about ghosts. She lives in Houston with feline overlords who like to "help" with her work. Her day job in law proves truth is stranger than fiction.

Check out some of the other Spooky America titles available now!

Spooky America was adapted from the creeptastic Haunted America series for adults. Haunted America explores historical haunts in cities and regions across America. Each book chronicles both the widely known and less-familiar history behind local ghosts and other unexplained mysteries. Here's more from the original *Ghosts of Old Town Albuquerque* author Cody Polston: